GRADE 1
Book 1

LANGUAGE SKILL BOOSTERS

George Moore

World Teachers Press®

Published with the permission of R.I.C. Publications Pty. Ltd.

First published by R.I.C. Publications Pty. Ltd., Perth, Western Australia.

Printed in the United States of America.

Order Number 2-5107
ISBN 1-58324-029-2

C D E F 03 02

Educational Resources
395 Main Street
Rowley, MA 01969
www.worldteacherspress.com

Language Skill Boosters – Level 1

Language Skill Boosters is a series of seven books for elementary and middle school years. Each work sheet deals with a language skill specific to that year level, making it easy to link the content to what has been taught in the classroom. Each set of exercises is followed by a review sheet which checks the concepts, skills and content covered in the previous work. The review sheet may be done as a test or as review exercises with the student able to look back at previous work. A combination of these approaches could be used.

The basic work on each sheet is followed by a "Challenge" section which is more difficult. Most words can be found in the abridged dictionaries common in elementary and middle schools but a few words in these "Challenge" sections may need reference to a more comprehensive dictionary. Answers have been provided for your convenience.

Most exercises have brief answers so the work can be completed easily and quickly.

An individual student record sheet has been provided to communicate progress to parents.

Contents

Introduction

Consolidation and review activities are recognized as an integral part of learning and understanding a specific concept. Once a concept has been taught, students need several opportunities to practice, develop and understand the ideas and methods behind it.

Language Skill Boosters provides exactly this opportunity. The reinforcement of concepts through an assignment approach allows you to readily evaluate where each student may be having difficulties and provides parents with the opportunity to see how their child is achieving in the area of language.

The thirty-six assignments and four review sheets follow the same format, allowing the student to focus solely on the task at hand. This also develops a routine which aids the learning process and allows the student to attack independent activities/homework with confidence.

Strategies

Language Skill Boosters can be used as:

1. *Consolidation of classwork*
    Once a concept has been presented in class, the appropriate assignment can be photocopied and completed in class to consolidate and reinforce the concept.

2. *Review of classwork*
    At the end of a unit of work, the assignments can be used to assess the students' understanding of a particular concept. This allows you to focus further instruction at the point of need for individual students. This approach also provides a straightforward approach to evaluation and recording of the student's understanding of language.

3. *Homework activities*
    Each assignment can be photocopied and sent home for students to complete independently over the course of the week or pre-designated time period. Parents/Guardians can assist the student if they are having difficulties. The following approaches are encouraged:
    (a)   Assist the student with the process involved without solving the problem for the student, and
    (b)   encourage the student to try to solve the problem.
    Any problems encountered at home should be discussed with you at the earliest possible convenience. Each assignment focuses on one concept and the questions show a varying degree of difficulty.

Instructions

The instructions provided on each assignment are clear and concise. Each instruction has been carefully written to avoid ambiguity. This allows students to work as independently as they have no need to clarify the question.

Benefits

The benefits of *Language Skill Boosters* are many.

1. You can readily evaluate where each student is having success or difficulties.

2. Provides parents with the opportunity to observe how their child is achieving in the area of language.

3. Opens communication between school and home regarding each student's progress.

4. Opportunities are provided for students to practice, consolidate and review various concepts treated in class.

5. Students are able to take some responsibility for their own learning.

Conclusion

Language Skill Boosters is a useful tool for developing the knowledge and understanding of a broad range of language concepts. Students can develop a high level of confidence with the opportunities they are given to consolidate what they learn. This confidence leads to success and a positive self-image.

Page	Concept	Date	Comment	Signature
7.	Initial Sounds			
8.	Initial Sounds			
9.	Final Sounds			
10.	Final Sounds			
11.	Sight Words			
12.	Words in the Environment			
13.	Describing Pictures			
14.	Middle Sounds			
15.	Sentence Matching			
16.	Review			
17.	Initial Blends			
18.	Following Directions			
19.	Rhyming Words			
20.	Activity Words			
21.	Words in the Environment			
22.	Yes or No			
23.	Read and Draw			
24.	Capital Letters and Periods			
25.	Opposites			
26.	Review			
27.	Pictorial News Story			
28.	Rhyming Words			
29.	Following Directions			
30.	Capital Letters			
31.	Word Categories			
32.	Listen and Draw			
33.	Describing Pictures			
34.	Plurals			
35.	Alphabet Search			
36.	Review			
37.	What Could I Be?			
38.	Final Blends			
39.	Opposites			
40.	Compound Words			
41.	Choose the Word			
42.	Similar Words			
43.	Sound Alikes			
44.	Word Categories			
45.	Alphabetical Order			
46.	Review			

Name: _____

1. Color the pictures that <u>begin</u> with the letter in the box.

f

r

l

b

w

d

Challenge!

1. Draw two things that <u>begin</u> with "p" on the back of this sheet.

Initial Sounds

1. Circle the beginning sound for each picture. Color the pictures.

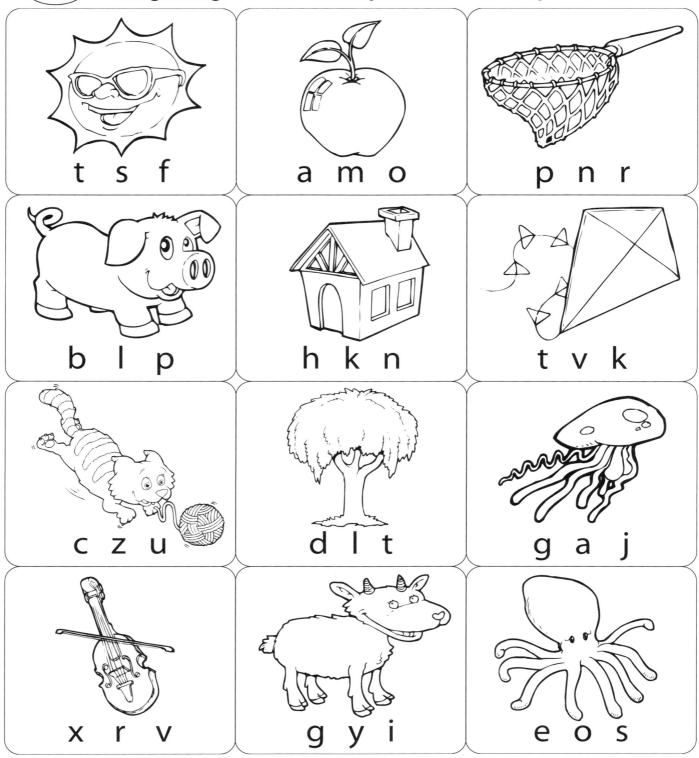

t s f

a m o

p n r

b l p

h k n

t v k

c z u

d l t

g a j

x r v

g y i

e o s

Challenge!

1. Cut out two pictures from a magazine or newspaper that begin with "d." Glue them on the back of this sheet.

Name: _____

1. Color the pictures that <u>end</u> with the letter in the box.

Challenge!

1. Draw two things that <u>end</u> with "g" on the back of this sheet.

Final Sounds

1. Circle the end sound for each picture. Color the pictures.

g m r

t e d

p n l

f d p

v c f

s h u

p j r

h n a

x d k

n v m

j x g

t g e

Challenge!

1. Cut out two pictures from a magazine or newspaper that <u>end</u> with "t." Glue them on the back of this sheet.

1. **Practice reading these words every day.**
   Color a box under the word when you have read it.

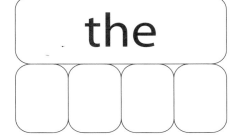

the

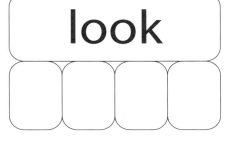

look

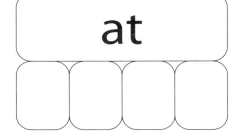

at

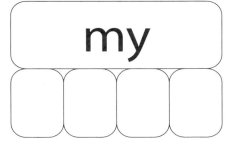

my

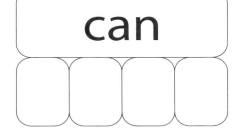

can

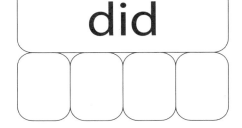

did

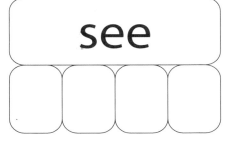

see

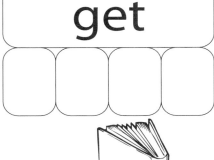

get

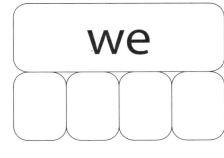

we

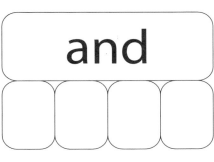

and

Challenge!

1. **Read and copy these words.**

yes _____   no _____

he _____   she _____

Words in the Environment

1. You will need some empty cereal boxes, cracker boxes, etc.
Find a word on the boxes to match the letters below.
Cut the words out and paste them in the box.

begins with "b"

begins with "w"

ends with "n"

ends with "d"

begins with "th"

has a "sh" in it

Challenge!

1. Find a word with ten letters. Paste below.

Describing Pictures

1. Look at the pictures below. Write a sentence about each one.

(a) _____

_____

_____

_____

_____

(b) _____

_____

_____

_____

Challenge!

1. Draw a picture of one of your toys. Write a sentence about it.

_____

_____

_____

_____

Middle Sounds

1. Color the pictures with the same <u>middle</u> sound as the one in the box.

a				
o				
e				

2. Circle the <u>middle</u> sound for each picture. Color the pictures.

a o u

i u o

e i a

a o e

Challenge!

1. Write the <u>middle</u> sound for these.

 _____

 _____

**1. Match the sentences to the correct picture.
Color the pictures.**

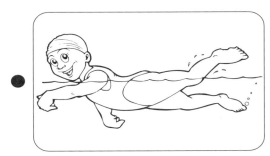

I am in bed. •

I can run. •

I have a cat. •

I can swim. •

Challenge!

1. Match the <u>beginning</u> of the sentence to the <u>ending</u>.

She can ride •   • a ball.

He has •   • to school.

She is going •   • a bike.

1. Color the pictures that <u>begin</u> with the letter in the box.

g				

2. Color the pictures that <u>end</u> with the letter in the box.

n				

3. Color the pictures with the same <u>middle</u> sound as the one in the box.

i				

4. Match the sentence to the picture.

He has a book.

She has a cat.

5. Color the box if you can read these words.

me ⬭   and ⬭

by ⬭   the ⬭

6. Find an empty cereal box or a magazine. Find two words which end with "t." Glue them on the back of this sheet.

7. Write a sentence about this picture.

Munch Munch Munch

_____

_____

_____

Initial Blends

1. Color the pictures that <u>begin</u> with the same sound as the one in the box.

dr

cl

tr

fl

2. Circle the <u>beginning</u> sound for each picture. Color the pictures.

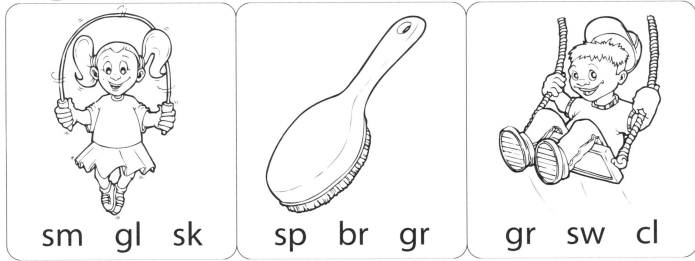

sm   gl   sk   sp   br   gr   gr   sw   cl

Challenge!

1. Write the <u>beginning</u> sound for these.

 _____og

 _____oom

Following Directions

Read the instructions at the bottom of the page, one at a time.
Students listen carefully and follow the instructions.

1. Listen and draw.

✏️ Color the umbrella green.

✏️ Draw a cloud in the sky.

✏️ Color the bucket red.

✏️ Draw a hat on the boy.

✏️ Draw a crab on the sand.

Challenge!

1. Read and draw.

✏️ Draw three shells on the sand castle in the beach picture.

✏️ Draw two birds in the sky in the beach picture.

Rhyming Words

1. Color the pictures that <u>rhyme</u> with the one in the box.

2. Draw a picture that <u>rhymes</u> with each word.

hot	peg	ten

Challenge!

1. Match the words that <u>rhyme</u>.

box •   • fog

wet •   • fox

log •   • jet

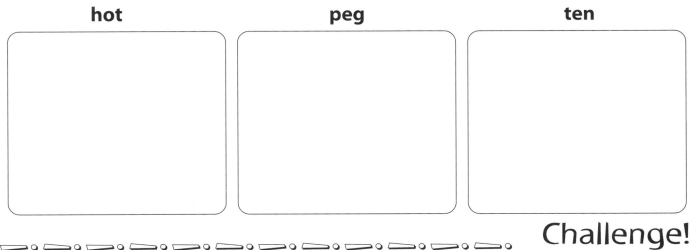

1. Write the word under the picture.

read	run	swim

_____ _____ _____

sing	skip	eat

_____ _____ _____

Challenge!

1. Draw a picture for these words.

sleep

hop

1. Look in your kitchen to make the following lists. Copy or write the word.

begins with "p" or "f"

ends with "t"

_____

_____

_____

has a "ch" in it

has six letters in it

_____

_____

_____

Challenge!

1. Cut out a label from a food you like.
Glue it on the back of this sheet.

Your food word ends with the letter _____.

Yes or No

1. Color yes or no.

(a) A ship is little.   yes   no

(b) An ant is big.   yes   no

(c) It is hot today.   yes   no

(d) An apple can be red.   yes   no

(e) A snake can fly.   yes   no

2. Write yes or no.

(a) Do you go to school? _____

(b) Can you run and jump? _____

(c) Are you six? _____

(d) Is your hair black? _____

(e) Do you have a pet? _____

(f) Can you count to ten? _____

Challenge!

1. Make up your own yes or no question.

_____

_____ yes   no

Name: _____

1. Read and draw.

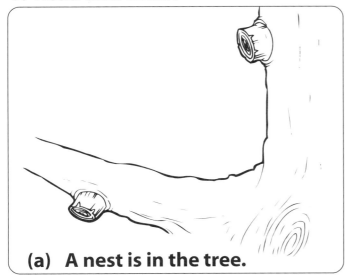

(a) **A nest is in the tree.**

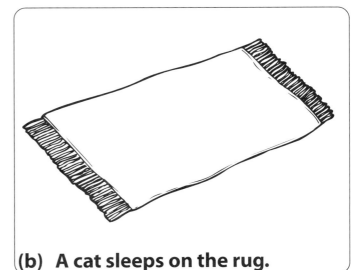

(b) **A cat sleeps on the rug.**

(c) **Two fish swim in the pond.**

Challenge!

1. Copy the missing word. Color the picture.

fish

dog

A brown _____ eats a bone.

1. **Read each sentence.**
   (Circle) the **capital letters** and **periods**.

(a) My hat is green.

(b) The wind blew the kite.

(c) A bird is in the sky.

> *A sentence must begin with a **capital letter**.*
> *A sentence must end with a **period**.*

2. **Read each sentence.**
   Put in the capital letters and periods.

(a) T /the sea is blue

(b) we have a red bucket

(c) there are two shells on the sand

(d) the sun is hot today

(e) we will go for a swim

Challenge!

1. **Write a sentence of your own.**
   Draw a picture.

_____

_____

_____

Name: _____

*Boy is the **opposite** of girl.*

1. Draw **opposites** for these. Finish the word.

little

happy

b_____g

s_____d

2. Match the **opposites**.

young •   • down

tall •   • old

up •   • cold

hot •   • short

────────────────────────────── **Challenge!**

1. Write the **opposite**.

yes _____   right _____

stop _____   up _____

1. Color the pictures that <u>begin</u> with the same sound as the one in the box.

br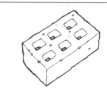

2. Color the pictures that <u>rhyme</u> with the word in the box.

men

3. Match the <u>opposites</u>.

stop •   • yes

big •   • down

no •   • little

happy •   • go

up •   • sad

4. Read and draw.

Two fish swim in a bowl.

5. Circle the <u>capital letters</u>.
   Put in a <u>period</u>.

A helmet is on Tim's head

Tim has a new bike

It is red and black

6. Color <u>yes</u> or <u>no</u>.

(a) A banana is red.

(b) It is cold today.

Pictorial News Story

1. Think about some news you would like to tell about yourself. Draw pictures to show <u>Who? What? When?</u> and <u>Where?</u> it happened. Use the pictures to tell someone about it.

Who?	What?
When?	Where?

Challenge!

1. Make up a news story about some news you would like to tell about someone in your family. Use a separate piece of paper.

Name: _____

1. Color each <u>rhyming</u> pair of words the same color.

sing   tree   band

long   me

hand   song   ring

sky   my

2. (Circle) the <u>rhyming</u> words.
Answer <u>yes</u> or <u>no</u>.

(a) Can a mouse live in a house? _____

(b) Can a bee live in a tree? _____

(c) Can a fish live in a dish? _____

(d) Can a cat live in a hat? _____

(e) Can a frog live in a log? _____

Challenge!

1. Write a <u>rhyming</u> word for these.

peg _____   glad _____

win _____   then _____

Name: _____

Read the instructions at the bottom of the page, one at a time.
Students listen carefully and follow the instructions.

1. Listen and draw.

✏️ Draw a ball next to the dog.

✏️ Draw a green hat on the boy.

✏️ Color the train red and black.

✏️ Color the girl's overalls yellow.

✏️ Color the boy's shorts black and blue.

✏️ Draw a picture of a house in the frame on the wall.

Challenge!

1. Read and draw.

✏️ Draw two more toys on the floor.

✏️ Color the boy's shirt with a color beginning with "g."

Name: _____

Hello. My name is Danny.

Hello. My name is Hannah.

Capital letters are used at the beginning of a sentence.
Capital letters are also used to begin our names.

What is your name? _____

**1. Read the names below.
Write each name with a <u>capital letter</u>.**

tim

_____

patch _____

mia

_____

socks _____

Challenge!

**1. Write a name for each
of these children.**

_____   _____

Word Categories

1. Read the **animal** words below.
Write them in the correct word shape.

dog   cow   sheep   cat   lion

Challenge!

1. Match the **animal** to its **young**.

cow •	• cub
dog •	• calf
sheep •	• kitten
cat •	• puppy
lion •	• lamb

Listen and Draw

Read the instructions at the bottom of the page, one at a time.
Students listen carefully and follow the instructions.

1. Finish the picture.

 Our boat is blue and white.

 The sun is shining in the sky.

 Dad has a big fish on his hook.

 Three little fish swim under the boat.

 A bird is on the boat.

Challenge!

1. Boats usually have a name. Name the boat in the picture. Write it below.

_____

Language Skill Boosters Book 1

Describing Pictures

1. Circle the word that best tells about the picture.

big   cute   hard

sad   happy   tall

soft   round   long

little   blue   mad

hot   small   cold

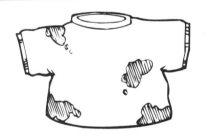

clean   dirty   hard

Challenge!

1. Write two words to tell about each picture.

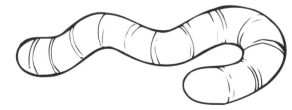

_____   _____

_____   _____

1. Rewrite these words adding "s" to make them say more than one.

book _____

truck _____

shoe _____

plum _____

brick _____

ant _____

2. Color the correct word.

(a) Two [snail] [snails] are on the leaf.

(b) There are lots of [flower] [flowers] in the garden.

(c) We have a new [girl] [girls] in our class.

(d) I like to eat fish and [chip] [chips] .

(e) That is my [bag] [bags] .

Challenge!

1. Fill in the missing number.

[ ] bananas

[ ] apples

[ ] orange

[ ] bowl

[ ] bunch of grapes

Name: _____

1. Can you think of an animal that <u>begins</u> with each letter of the alphabet? Write the word in the space below. Choose five animals and draw their picture on the back of this page.

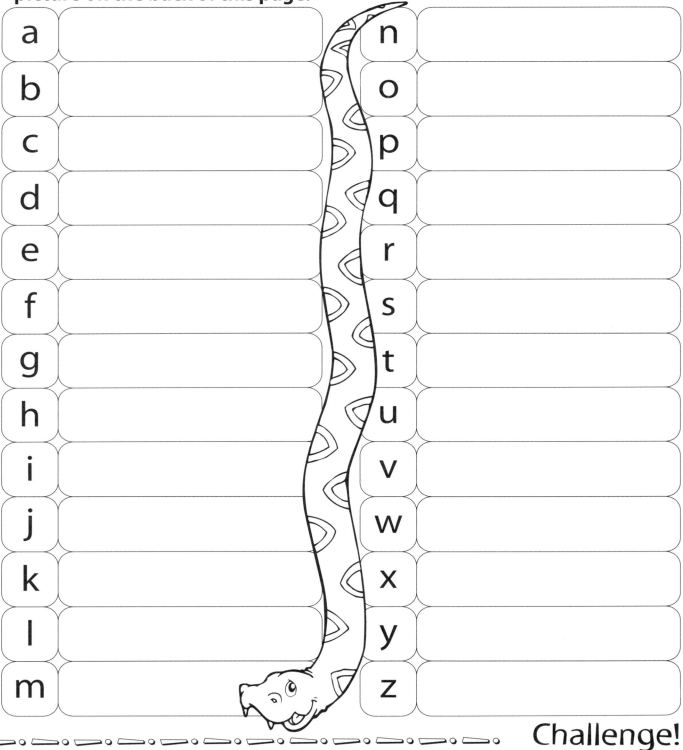

a		n	
b		o	
c		p	
d		q	
e		r	
f		s	
g		t	
h		u	
i		v	
j		w	
k		x	
l		y	
m		z	

Challenge!

1. See if you can think of another animal for each letter of the alphabet.

1. Match the <u>rhyming</u> words.

hop •   • wet

get •   • chip

lip •   • shop

2. Write a <u>rhyming</u> word.

cat _____

pin _____

3. Write your name. Remember to use a <u>capital letter</u>.

_____

4. Write these numbers in the correct word shape.

three   seven   four

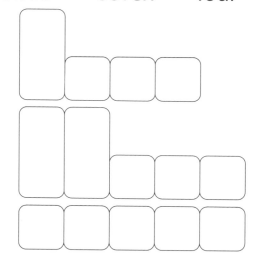

5. Color the correct word.

(a) The dog has a | bone | | bones | .

(b) Is that your | book | | books | ?

(c) Three | egg | | eggs | were in the nest.

6. Think of two animals that <u>begin</u> with "b." Write a word or draw a picture.

_____   _____

7. Listen/Read and draw.

Three cars are on the road. One car is green. The other cars are blue.

What Could I Be?

I am round.
I can bounce.
Draw me.

I am a _____.

I can swim.
I live in the sea.
Draw me.

I am a _____.

I am tall.
I have leaves.
Draw me.

I am a _____.

I can fly.
I lay eggs.
Draw me.

I am a _____.

Challenge!

1. Make up your own "What am I?"

I am _____.

I have _____.

I can _____.

I am _____.

2. Draw me on the back of this sheet.

Final Blends

1. Cut out the pictures below and glue them under the correct <u>end</u> sound.

nt	mp	nd

Challenge!

1. Draw another picture or write a word for each <u>end</u> sound in the boxes below.

nt	mp	nd

Name:_____

Happy is the opposite of sad.

1. Match the opposites.

wet •   • thin

fat •   • shut

open •   • in

out •   • dry

2. Draw the opposite for these. Finish the word.

night

_____ay

hot

_____old

Challenge!

1. Write the word that is the opposite.

Mom   over   her   fast

slow _____   Dad _____

under _____   him _____

Compound Words

A **compound word** is two words joined together.

1. Write the compound word.

egg   +   cup   = _____

tooth   +   brush   = _____

rain   +   bow   = _____

foot   +   ball   = _____

2. Match the compound words to the picture.

beanbag   seaweed   popcorn   goldfish

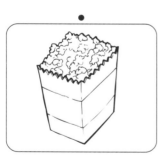   

Challenge!

1. Circle the compound words. Color yes or no.

(a) Have you made a snowman?   yes   no

(b) Can you eat a basketball?   yes   no

1. Write the correct word to complete each sentence.

 hit    walk    wash    ride    fly

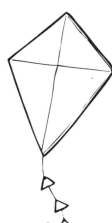

(a) We help Dad to _____ the car.

(b) Do you know how to _____ a bike?

(c) The boy _____ the ball with his bat.

(d) A kite can _____ in the sky.

(e) I like to _____ my dog in the park.

2. Color the correct word.

(a) We | get | | have | a pet bird.

(b) Can you | see | | look | the funny clown?

(c) Have you | do | | done | your work?

(d) Please | give | | put | the book to me.

(e) Is | this | | they | your bag?

Challenge!

1. Circle the odd one out.

blue   green   apple   red

horse   pig   cow   girl

Name: _____

Go and start are words that have nearly the same meaning.

1. Match the words which have almost the same meaning.

small •   • fast

high •   • little

street •   • tidy

quick •   • tall

neat •   • road

2. Circle the words which have almost the same meaning.

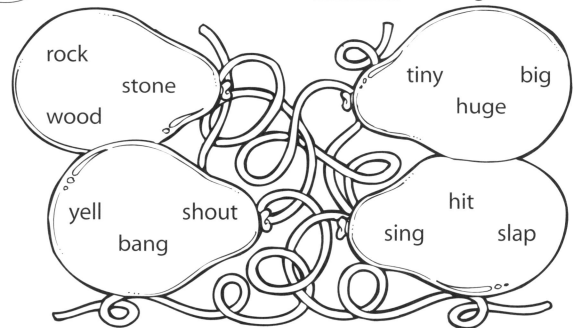

rock   stone   wood

tiny   big   huge

yell   shout   bang

hit   sing   slap

Challenge!

1. Choose the correct word to fit in the word shape.

fix – mend

smile – grin

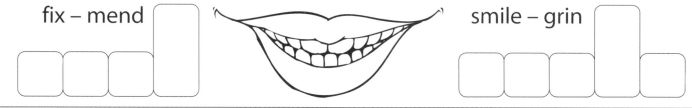

Sound Alikes

Sometimes words **sound alike** but have different spelling.
For example, **for** and **four**.

1. Draw a picture of the word that __sounds like__ these.

son	sun	tale	tail

2. Write the correct word.

see · sea · for · four

(a) Would you like to go _____ a walk?

(b) There were _____ eggs in the nest.

(c) I can _____ a bird in the tree.

(d) Fish live in the _____.

Challenge!

1. Draw a picture and write a word that __sounds like__ these.

meet	be

Word Categories

1. Circle the word that doesn't belong.
Write or draw another word for each one.

(a) Things you can eat.

ice cream   apple   sand

sandwich   cheese

_____

(b) Things you can wear.

hat   T-shirt   shoe

umbrella   jumper

_____

(c) Things that are small.

ant   mouse   lion

kitten   fly

_____

(d) Things found in the sea.

shark   whale   seaweed

elephant   crab

_____

Challenge!

1. Check all the things that can be green. On the back of this page write or draw something else that can be green.

 apple ☐

 broccoli ☐

 strawberry ☐

 grass ☐

 leaves ☐

 grapes ☐

 carrot ☐

meat ☐

Name: _____

1. Write the names of these foods in **alphabetical order**.

banana   egg   donut

apple   cake

_____
_____
_____
_____
_____

2. Write each list of words in **alphabetical order**.

lion _____

tiger _____

zebra _____

horse _____

green _____

yellow _____

orange _____

pink _____

Challenge!

1. Write these words in **alphabetical order**.

(a) _____

(b) _____

(c) _____

(d) _____

(e) _____

car   ship   truck   van   bike

Name: _____

1. What am I?

I am in the sky.

I am hot.

I am the _____. Draw me.

2. Color the pictures which end with the sound in the box.

3. Circle the words which mean the same.

happy   glad   mean   jolly

4. Draw and write the opposite for these.

girl   Dad

5. Color the correct word.

(a) A [rainbow] [football] is pretty.

(b) A [be] [bee] can buzz.

(c) We like to swim in the [see] [sea].

6. Write these fruits in alphabetical order.

pear   banana   orange

Answers

pages 7-14
Teacher check all activities

Challenge!
1. Teacher check

page 15 Sentence Matching
1. Teacher check

Challenge!
1. She can ride a bike. He has a ball. She is going to school.

pages 16-18
Teacher check all activities

Challenge!
1. Teacher check

page 19 Rhyming Words
1.-2. Teacher check

Challenge!
1. box–fox, wet–jet, log–fog

pages 20-21
Teacher check all activities

Challenge!
1. Teacher check

page 22 Yes or No
1. (a) no   (b) no   (c) Teacher check
   (d) yes   (e) no
2. (a) yes   (b) – (d) Teacher check

Challenge!
1. Teacher check

page 23 Read and Draw
1. Teacher check

Challenge!
1. dog

page 24 Capital Letters and Periods
1.–2. Teacher check

Challenge!
1. Teacher check

page 25 Opposites
1. little–big, happy–sad
2. young–old, tall–short, up–down, hot–cold

Challenge!
1. yes–no, right–left, stop–go, up–down

page 26 Review
1.–2. Teacher check
3. stop–go, big–little, no–yes, happy–sad, up–down
4.–5. Teacher check
6. (a) no   (b) Teacher check

pages 27–30
Teacher check all activities

Challenge!
1. Teacher check

page 31 Word Categories
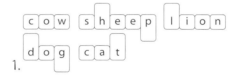
1.

Challenge!
1. cow–calf, dog–puppy, sheep–lamb, cat–kitten, lion–cub

pages 32–33
Teacher check all activities

Challenge!
1. Teacher check

page 34 Plurals
1. book–books, truck–trucks, shoe–shoes, plum–plums, brick–bricks, ant–ants
2. (a) snails (b) flowers (c) girl (d) chips (e) bag

Challenge!
1. two bananas, three apples, one orange, one bowl, one bunch of grapes

page 35 Alphabet Search
1. Teacher check

Challenge!
1. Teacher check

page 36 Review
1. hop–shop, get–wet, lip–chip
2.–3. Teacher check
4.

5. (a) bone (b) book (c) eggs
6.–7. Teacher check

page 37 What Could I Be?
Teacher check

Challenge!
1. Teacher check

page 38 Final Blends
1. Teacher check

Challenge!
1. Teacher check

page 39 Opposites
1. wet–dry, fat–thin, open–shut, out–in
2. night–day, hot–cold

Challenge!
1. slow–fast, under–over, Dad–Mom, him–her

page 40 Compound Words
1. Teacher check

Challenge!
1. Teacher check

page 41 Choose the Word
1. (a) wash (b) ride (c) hit (d) fly   (e) walk
2. (a) have (b) see (c) done (d) give (e) this

Challenge!
1. apple, girl

Answers

page 42 Similar Words
1. small–little, high–tall, street–road, quick–fast, neat–tidy
2. (a) rock–stone (b) big–huge
   (c) yell–shout (d) hit–slap

Challenge!
1.

page 43 Sound Alikes
1. Teacher check
2. (a) for (b) four (c) see (d) sea

Challenge!
1. meet–meat, be–bee

page 44 Word Categories
1. (a) sand (b) umbrella
   (c) lion (d) elephant

Challenge!
1. apple, broccoli, grass, leaves, grapes

page 45 Alphabetical Order
1. apple, banana, cake, donut, egg
2. horse, lion, tiger, zebra, green, orange, pink, yellow

Challenge!
1. (a) bike (b) car (c) ship (d) truck (e) van

page 46 Review
1. sun
2. Teacher check
3. happy, glad, jolly
4. girl–boy, Dad–Mom
5. (a) rainbow (b) bee (c) sea
6. banana, orange, pear